DISCARD

THE
STORY *of*
THE STATUE
of LIBERTY

A HISTORY PERSPECTIVES BOOK

Annie Qaiser

Published in the United States of America by Cherry Lake Publishing
Ann Arbor, Michigan
www.cherrylakepublishing.com

Consultants: Robert J. Allison, PhD, Chair and Professor, Department of
History, Suffolk University; Marla Conn, ReadAbility, Inc.
Editorial direction: Red Line Editorial
Book design and illustration: Sleeping Bear Press

Photo Credits: Library of Congress, cover (left), 1 (left), 4, 14, 18, 22;
Agence Papyrus/AP Images, cover (middle), 1 (middle), 7, 12, 21;
Photodisc/Thinkstock, cover (right), 1 (right), 29; Albert Fernique/Library
of Congress, 10; Musee Bartholdi/AP Images, 15; AP Images, 25; AIP/AP
Images, 27; Jack E. Boucher/Library of Congress, 30

Library of Congress Cataloging-in-Publication Data
Qaiser, Annie, 1983-
  The story of the Statue of Liberty / Annie Qaiser.
    pages cm. – (Perspectives library)
  ISBN 978-1-62431-422-3 (hardcover) – ISBN 978-1-62431-498-8 (pbk.)
– ISBN 978-1-62431-460-5 (pdf) – ISBN 978-1-62431-536-7 (ebook)
1. Statue of Liberty (New York, N.Y.)–Juvenile literature. 2. New York
(N.Y.)–Buildings, structures, etc.–Juvenile literature. I. Title.
F128.64.L6Q35 2013
974.7'1–dc23

                          2013006436

Cherry Lake Publishing would like to acknowledge the work of
The Partnership for 21st Century Skills. Please visit www.p21.org
for more information.

Printed in the United States of America
Corporate Graphics Inc.
July 2013
CLFA11

TABLE OF CONTENTS

In this book, you will read about the story of the Statue of Liberty from three perspectives. Each perspective is based on real things that happened to real people who helped build or reported on the Statue of Liberty. As you'll see, the same event can look different depending on one's point of view.

1

Armand Luc-Cardell

French Artisan

In 1876, construction of the Statue of Liberty began. We artisans were at the **foundry** of Gaget, Gaulthier & Co. in Paris, France, to start the work. The dream to build the Statue of Liberty began several years ago, in 1865. Another artisan told me artist Frédéric-Auguste Bartholdi attended a party with other influential Frenchmen. They discussed the United States and its upcoming **centennial** birthday on July 4, 1876. The date would mark 100 years since America signed the Declaration of Independence. The group thought it would be great if France gave the United States a gift for this occasion. It would honor the country's freedom and celebrate the friendship between France and the United States.

ANALYZE THIS

▶ Find another chapter that discusses the meaning behind the Statue of Liberty. How does that perspective compare to this perspective?

Monsieur Bartholdi wanted to make a huge monument as a gift. He sketched and drew until he came up with the creation. The statue would be of a woman wearing robes and a crown. She would represent Libertas, the Roman goddess of freedom. Her right arm would be raised in the air. She would hold a torch in her right hand. The statue's left hand would hold a tablet with the date of the country's independence, July 4, 1776. In 1875, Bartholdi made a four-foot statue out of clay. This would be the design for the larger statue. He also began working with a committee called the Franco-American Union to raise money to build the statue.

Monsieur Bartholdi and we artisans first made a nine-foot statue based on the four-foot statue. Then we created a 36-foot statue as a larger model. At last we began work on the final 151-foot statue. We sectioned the statue into smaller parts because it was so large. This way we could work on several parts at the same time. Monsieur Bartholdi watched to make sure we formed each piece of the massive structure correctly.

After the right arm and torch were completed, they were packed and shipped to the United States. They were going to be showcased at the Centennial **Exposition** in Philadelphia, Pennsylvania, in August 1876. Our American friends then saw just how large the gift from the people of France would be.

▲ *Many artisans worked on each part of the statue, including the right hand and torch.*

We hoped the Americans could tell we were honoring our friendship with the magnificent gift.

Many French people supported Bartholdi's gift to the United States. However, some were against it. They believed the Americans did not appreciate the symbolic gift of the Statue of Liberty. If they did, they would have done more to raise money for the project.

We began work on the head and shoulders next. Like all the workers and artisans, I worked with extreme concentration and precise measurements. If any of the smaller sections were off by even one centimeter, the entire structure would have to be rebuilt.

Carpenters worked on the large wooden pieces that were used to shape the metal of the statue. They sawed and sanded narrow pieces of wood to shape them into a giant mold. Plaster was poured to create molds from the wood frames. Then the metal workers covered the frames with thin sheets of copper. They hammered the copper against the wood frames until it took on the shape of the mold. The work was messy. Everything and everyone in the foundry was covered in sawdust and plaster dust.

The copper sheets are thin. Yet they are strong enough to withstand the wind, water, and salty air they will face in New York Harbor. This is where the statue will be placed. The copper will **oxidize** to form a bluish-green layer. This layer will actually stop the

SWAYING STATUE

The copper sheets used to build the monument are the thickness of two pennies. The copper sheets are nailed onto the frame. This allows the structure to move freely with the direction of the wind, which can blow at a rate of up to 50 miles per hour in the harbor. This causes the statue to sway up to three inches. The torch and flame can sway up to six inches.

rest of the copper-covered statue from **decaying**. This was one reason Monsieur Bartholdi chose copper sheets for the outside of the statue. The sheets will also be easier and lighter to transport across the Atlantic.

In July 1878, the **bust** of the statue was finished. It was placed on display at the Paris Universal Exposition. Visitors paid a small fee to go inside the statue. This helped raise funds needed to complete the rest of the statue. The French people were in awe of the massive metal structure. To many, it stands for the strong support the French have given America over the years. We were proud to make this symbolic statue.

◀ *The bust of the Statue of Liberty was displayed in Paris.*

By 1880, Gustave Eiffel had built the 98-foot structure that would support the statue. This skeleton is made of iron. In 1882, Monsieur Bartholdi decided to assemble the statue in Parc Monceau, a public park in Paris. The workers used the iron structure that Eiffel made as a base. They built the statue right in the park because there was no indoor space tall enough to contain the statue once it was completed. This way the French people could continue to admire the artistic abilities of their countrymen. They could watch as the statue was being built. The workers laid copper sheets, piece by piece, over the wood and iron skeleton. The French referred to the statue as the Lady of the Park.

By 1884, we were nearly done creating the monument. But we learned the Americans were just beginning to build the **pedestal** that the statue will rest on. We continued with our work. Soon the copper sheets were fully attached to the skeleton. We had completed the statue. The massive Statue of Liberty stood by itself.

But unfortunately, our friends in America were not yet ready to receive our gift. Monsieur Bartholdi was irate and frustrated. The Americans were lagging behind on the pedestal due to lack of funds. The work on the pedestal was only half completed.

It is spring of 1885 now. The monument has stood for months in Parc Monceau. But Monsieur Bartholdi has just given us orders to take the monument apart. The Americans are nearly ready

◀ *The Statue of Liberty stood in the Parc Monceau in Paris until it was ready to be sent to the United States.*

for the statue. We pack the copper sheets and frames into carefully labeled crates. On May 21, 1885, the crates are packed and on their way to the United States aboard the French Navy ship *Isère*.

From idea to fundraising to building, it has taken eight long years to create the statue. But our work is finally complete. The statue will need to be reassembled in the United States once the pedestal is done. We are proud of this monument. The statue represents harmony and liberty—characteristics we hope to share with the Americans for years to come.

THINK ABOUT IT

▶ What is the main idea of this chapter? Find two pieces of evidence that support the idea.

Sammy Rafe

American Harbor Worker

In late 1883, a buzz started to grow in New York City. People in the city were talking about a gigantic pedestal my fellow laborers and I were building on an island in the harbor. The pedestal was going to be built to survive the salty ocean air and fierce winds of New York Harbor. It also needed to support the weight of the statue that would rest upon it.

The French decided to present our country, the United States, with a large monument that symbolizes the friendship between America and France. It would also stand for the American dream of liberty and freedom for all.

In 1871, the French sculptor Frédéric-Auguste Bartholdi came from France to find the perfect location for the statue. He chose Fort Wood on Bedloe's Island. The tiny island is in the middle of the New York Harbor, near the mouth of the Hudson River. The statue would be the first thing ships would see when

Frédéric-Auguste Bartholdi chose Bedloe's Island in New York Harbor as the location for the statue. ▶

coming into New York Harbor. It would also be seen from the surrounding states. In 1876, the American Committee was created to raise funds for the monument's pedestal. In 1884, the statue was completed in France.

A GIFT

The French sculptor Frédéric-Auguste Bartholdi is known for creating the Statue of Liberty. But it was his teacher, Edouard de Laboulaye, who proposed the idea. Laboulaye wanted the Americans to receive a gift that celebrated French-American friendship and the United States' 100 years of freedom. The Statue of Liberty has broken chains and shackles around the feet. They stand for breaking free from harsh rule. The United States broke free from harsh rule before it was its own country. The French also did this during their revolution in 1787.

We had a lot of work to do on the pedestal yet, which meant jobs and money for us. Hundreds of **immigrant** workers provided the muscles and skills for the job. On August 5, 1884, we laid the first stone of the pedestal. The hours were long. We worked hard from dawn to dusk.

We dug a deep area into Bedloe's Island to create a strong foundation for the pedestal. We placed bricks and mortar to build a base 15 feet deep. It would withstand the intense winds that come off the Atlantic Ocean.

Our supervisor on the job took orders from General Charles P. Stone, the chief engineer of the project. Stone was in charge of making sure the pedestal was completed on time. But we ran into delays because money was running out.

SECOND SOURCE

▶ Find another source that describes the work done to prepare for the Statue of Liberty's arrival. How does it compare to the information you read here?

The American Committee was asking wealthy Americans to donate money to the project. The effort was not paying off though. Many Americans believed if the French were giving the gift, then they should pay for all of it—including the pedestal.

We were about halfway done with the pedestal in 1885. This was when I began to hear rumors that the work on the pedestal was going to stop. The money raised by the committee had dried up. Some newspapers wrote about how important the statue is. The *World* newspaper began a campaign to raise money to complete the pedestal.

◀ *People could see the progress on the pedestal's construction.*

I didn't have much to spare, but I sent in a few cents. I hoped I could help raise the money needed to keep building the pedestal. Working on this monument had been very important to me.

My family, like many other immigrants, chose to live in New York because it was our first home. My family came to the United States when I was a young boy. We were escaping poverty and famine in Ireland. But my parents also wanted to live in a land of liberty and freedom. The monument stands for these things. To me, working on this monument is a way to honor the country that has allowed my family to live a better life.

But it seemed the fundraising didn't do much good. We had to stop working for a while. Soon enough, though, Stone called us back to work again. All those people who sent in a few dollars and cents helped raise a large sum of money. Work on the pedestal project could begin again.

On June 17, 1885, the ship *Isère* arrived from France. It contained the Statue of Liberty. The statue had been taken apart and stored in hundreds of boxes aboard the ship. The crates were put into storage because the statue couldn't be rebuilt until we finished the pedestal. We worked even harder and faster to complete our job.

Now it is the spring of 1886. We have just laid the last brick of the pedestal. At 154 feet tall, the pedestal is massive. The poured concrete walls are 20 feet thick. The outside walls have a **facade** of granite.

Immigrant workers have started working on the iron skeleton that will support the copper sheets of the Statue of Liberty. Soon, workers will unpack the stored crates. Metal workers and artisans will assemble the statue. The people of the United

THINK ABOUT IT

▶ What information did you learn about the Statue of Liberty that you did not know before? What facts surprised you?

States of America will then see the results of the hard labor and devotion of hundreds of people—French and American—to make liberty stand tall.

◀ Once the pedestal was completed, the assembly of the Statue of Liberty began.

Ashley Pensley
American Reporter

I work under Joseph Pulitzer. He is the **publisher** and owner of the newspaper the *World*. Being a reporter has taught me much about the power of the written word. Not only do reporters tell the news, but we can make a difference with the stories we tell.

In March 1885, all those involved in the newspaper started working on a five-month campaign to raise money for a pedestal. The campaign consisted of articles and editorials published in the *World*. It also included theater shows, dances, sporting events, recitals, and art shows throughout New York City.

A few years ago, the French decided to give the American people a gift to show the strong bond between the French and American people. The gift would be a huge statue that would stand on Bedloe's Island. The French began creating the monument. We would build the pedestal on which the statue would be placed. The French completed their monument and presented it to Levi Morton, the American ambassador to France, on July 4, 1884. Unfortunately, the American Committee in charge of funding the pedestal ran out of money. The pedestal was only half complete.

ANALYZE THIS

▶ Find another chapter that discusses the difficulty of funding the Statute of Liberty project. How are the two perspectives similar? How are they different?

In the March 16, 1885 issue, the *World* printed a message for the people of the United States. The article told readers about the incomplete state of the pedestal. It would be a public humiliation and national disgrace if the Statue of Liberty arrived and the pedestal was nowhere near done. The newspaper reminded the American people that the French—workers, artists, shopkeepers, and merchants—paid to make the statue for us. Now, it was the American public's responsibility to fund the pedestal.

Our newspaper did not ask the wealthy to **contribute** the remainder of the funds. This was because they had their chance to donate money in the previous months before the campaign began. They did not donate very much. Pulitzer attacked the wealthy for being stingy and the middle class for depending on the rich. We asked the working class and average American citizens to send in whatever they could afford. We would print the names of all contributors in

Joseph Pulitzer played a key role in fundraising for the pedestal. ▶

the papers. It didn't matter who the person was or how much they donated. Their names and contributions would be printed.

Pulitzer himself started the campaign by donating $250 to the cause. Donations poured in over the next few weeks. People donated from as little as a few pennies to amounts as large as a thousand dollars.

In about five months, we printed the names of about 125,000 donors from all over the country. They helped raise the extra funds needed to finish the pedestal. By August 11, 1885, the *World* was proud to have helped raise $100,000. The power of the written word is strong, indeed.

"THE NEW COLOSSUS"

On November 2, 1883, Emma Lazarus wrote the poem "The New Colossus" to welcome new immigrants to the United States. Lazarus donated the poem to an art auction to raise money for the pedestal fund. In 1903, her poem was engraved on a plaque and placed inside the pedestal of the Statue of Liberty, where there is space for visitors. Her powerful words touched the hearts of those who had left their homeland for a better life:

Give me your tired, your poor, / Your huddled masses yearning to breathe free, / The wretched refuse of your teeming shore. / Send these, the homeless, tempest-tost to me, / I lift my lamp beside the golden door!

For the next eight months, workers rushed to complete the pedestal. In April 1886, metal workers and carpenters took over. They worked quickly to

▲ *Once enough funds were raised, construction on the pedestal began again.*

assemble the statue on the pedestal. By the fall of 1886, the Statue of Liberty rose majestically from its stone base. It towers 305 feet above Bedloe's Island, from the ground all the way to the torch. While the statue was being assembled, the French flag covered Lady Liberty's face to keep an element of surprise.

Today, October 28, 1886, is the official unveiling of *Liberty Enlightening the World*. This is the statue's official name. The creator of the statue, Frédéric-Auguste Bartholdi, is here to do the honors. One million New Yorkers are here to witness the event. The Statue of Liberty represents liberty and justice. These two qualities define our country today and will continue to do so for the future.

SECOND SOURCE

▶ Find another source that describes when the Statue of Liberty was unveiled. How does that source compare to the information you read here?

▲ *Today, the Statue of Liberty continues to be a symbol of freedom around the world.*

LOOK, LOOK AGAIN

This image shows the broken chains and shackles that are around the Statue of Liberty's feet.

1. Imagine you are an artisan working on the statue. Why do you think the chains and shackles are a part of the statue?

2. Imagine you are a worker constructing the pedestal. What would you think when you saw this part of the statue for the first time?

3. Imagine you are a reporter. How would you describe this image in an article?

GLOSSARY

bust (BUHST) the head, neck, and shoulders of a statue

centennial (sen-TEN-ee-uhl) the 100th-year celebration of an event

contribute (kuhn-TRIB-yoot) to give money to reach a goal

decay (di-KAY) to break down or rot

exposition (ek-spoh-ZIH-shuhn) a public show

facade (fuh-SAHD) the front of a building or structure

foundry (FOUN-dree) a place where metals are melted and shaped

immigrant (IM-i-gruhnt) someone who moves to a new country from another

oxidize (AHK-si-dize) to go through a chemical change when exposed to oxygen

pedestal (PED-i-stuhl) the base of a statue

publisher (PUHB-lish-ur) a person in charge of a newspaper or other company that prints and publishes material

LEARN MORE

Further Reading

Malam, John. *You Wouldn't Want to Be a Worker on the Statue of Liberty!: A Monument You'd Rather Not Build.* New York: Franklin Watts, 2009.

Mann, Elizabeth. *Statue of Liberty: A Tale of Two Countries.* New York: Miyaka Press, 2011.

Rappaport, Doreen. *Lady Liberty: A Biography.* Cambridge, MA: Candlewick Press, 2008.

Web Sites

The Light of Liberty
http://kids.nationalgeographic.com/kids/stories/history/statue-of-liberty/
This Web site describes the history and significance of the Statue of Liberty.

Statue of Liberty
http://www.nps.gov/stli/forkids/index.htm
The National Park Service offers interesting facts about the Statue of Liberty on this Web site.

INDEX

ABOUT THE AUTHOR

Annie Qaiser is a freelance writer. She lives in Minnesota with her family.